MW01139413

# HOW DOES ALLAH LOOK?

## CHILDREN'S FIRST QUESTIONS

Written & Illustrated by Emma Apple

For Hend

Copyright © 2015 Emma Apple

Published by Books by Emma Apple – Chicago IL USA
All rights reserved. This book or any portion thereof may not be reproduced or used in any manner
without the express written permission of the copyright holder.

First Edition - 2017 Update.

ISBN-13: 978-0692380864

www.emmaapple.com

# BISMILLAH AR-RAHMAN AR-RAHEEM
# WITH GOD'S NAME

The aim of this book is to encourage children to think about the unseen and to know that, while their imagination is vast, it is also limited, and Allah is different from all they know and all they imagine.

We hope that this will help children and their families to know their creator and to look closer at the natural world to understand Him.

# HOW DOES ALLAH LOOK?

There are many kinds of living things
in the world.

All kinds of plants from flowers to trees, all kinds
of creatures from insects to birds, and humans
from every place in the world.

Do you know how all of them look?

The world is full of places humans haven't yet explored.

Oceans, deserts and huge forests.

Can you imagine everything that may be hidden there?

Things exist in our huge universe and even on our own little planet, that we don't know about or cannot see.

There are creatures deep in the oceans and forests that we have not discovered yet.

There are tiny organisms living all around us that we don't even know are there.

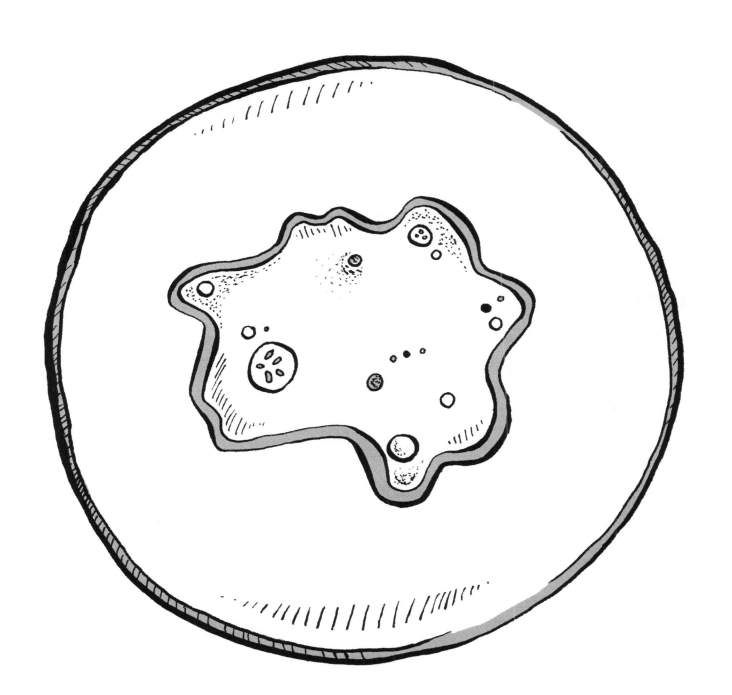

We often try to imagine how all these mysterious things might look.

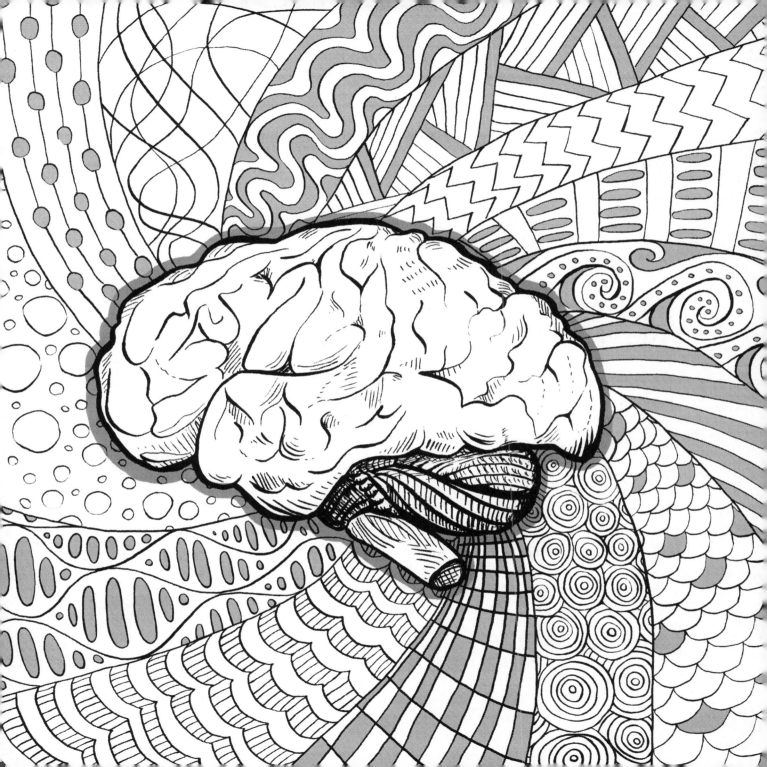

We even think up weird and wonderful fantasy creatures, like dragons, unicorns and monsters, that we know do not exist.

Even though it seems like we can imagine anything, we cannot imagine everything.

Our eyes were not designed to see every light, and our ears were not designed to hear every sound, but only the ones we need to communicate and survive.

In this same way, our brain was not designed to imagine how Allah looks.

Although we may not be able to know how Allah looks now, Allah has promised that those who know and follow Him, will see Him in Jannah (Heaven).

**In the Qur'an (6:103) Allah says that He has not given us the ability to know how he looks.**

*"No vision can grasp Him, but His grasp is over all vision; and He is the Subtle, the Acquainted with all things."*

**And in a Hadith Qudsi, Allah says that those in Jannah will not have the same limits.**

*"Then He will grant them that which no eye has seen, no ear has heard, and it has not crossed the mind of any human."*

# FROM THE QUR'AN

Prophet Musa (Moses) peace be upon him, once asked to see Allah. This is mentioned in the Qur'an, Surah 7, Ayah 143

*"And when Moses arrived at Our appointed time and his Lord spoke to him, he said, 'My Lord, show me (Yourself) that I may look at You.' (Allah) said, 'You will not see Me, but look at the mountain; if it should remain in place, then you will see Me.' But when his Lord appeared to the mountain, He rendered it level, and Moses fell unconscious. And when he awoke, he said, 'Exalted are You! I have repented to You, and I am the first of the believers.'"*

We call Allah "Him" because we don't have enough words to describe who or what Allah is, but Allah is different from all creation, male or female.

# BEYOND HUMAN VISION

Light is a kind of wave and is measured on a scale known as the Electromagnetic Spectrum. The light waves that the human eye can see make up less than 1% of the electromagnetic spectrum and are known as Visible Light. You may have heard of Infrared, Ultraviolet and X-Rays, these are some of the light waves on the electromagnetic spectrum that we can't see without special tools. We make use of these light waves in different ways. For example: remote control devices use infrared light to connect, ultraviolet lights are used to kill germs and X-ray machines let you see your bones.

Some creatures can see light waves that we can't. For example: some butterflies, birds, and fish can see UV light and some snakes see infrared light.

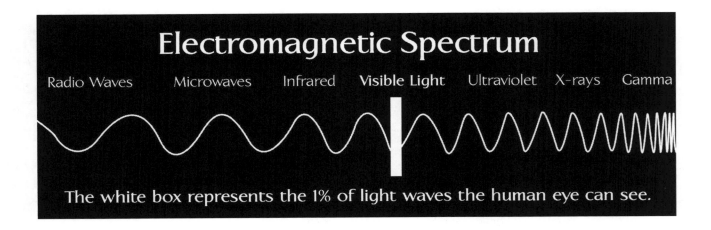

Electromagnetic Spectrum

Radio Waves    Microwaves    Infrared    **Visible Light**    Ultraviolet    X-rays    Gamma

The white box represents the 1% of light waves the human eye can see.

# BEYOND HUMAN HEARING

Sounds are a kind of wave just like light and are measured by frequency. Humans can hear frequencies between 20 and 20,000 Hz (hertz). There are also sounds around us that are higher frequency than we can hear, which is known as Ultrasonic and sounds that are lower frequency than we can hear, known as Infrasonic.

Some creatures can hear sound waves that we can't. Whales, elephants and some birds make and hear infrasonic sound and several kinds of moths and bats can make and hear ultrasonic sounds.

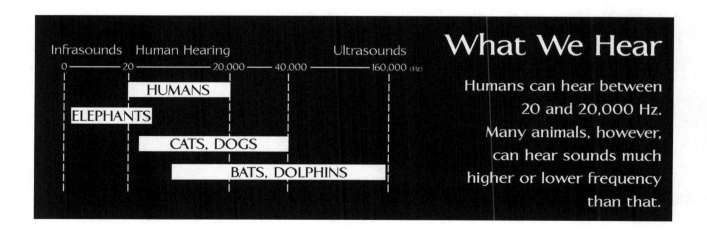

Infrasounds    Human Hearing                    Ultrasounds
0 —— 20 ———— 20,000 —— 40,000 ———— 160,000 (Hz)

HUMANS
ELEPHANTS
CATS, DOGS
BATS, DOLPHINS

## What We Hear

Humans can hear between 20 and 20,000 Hz. Many animals, however, can hear sounds much higher or lower frequency than that.

# WHAT WE KNOW, SO FAR...

Astronomers have only described about 1% of the observable universe and mapped about 50% of our tiny Solar System.

Here on our planet, Earth, there are about 1.2 million species known to science, and an estimated 8.7 million that are still unknown. Studies suggest that scientists have described less than 15% of living things on Earth.

Oceans cover 70% of the Earth and so far humans have only explored 5%. We have better maps of the Moon and Mars than of our Ocean floors.

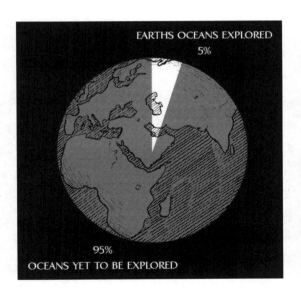

EARTHS OCEANS EXPLORED
5%

95%
OCEANS YET TO BE EXPLORED

SPECIES KNOWN TO SCIENCE
15%

85%
SPECIES NOT YET KNOWN TO SCIENCE

# GLOSSARY

**Allah** - The One God, The Creator.

**Exist** - Something that is, something that lives or has been created.

**Creatures** - Animals, living things.

**Organism** - A living animal, plant or single-celled life form.

**Universe** - All existing things in space. Planets, Galaxies, Stars and everything that has been created.

**Imagine** - To make a picture in your mind of something real or pretend.

**Mysterious** - Difficult or impossible to understand or explain.

**Fantasy** - Imaginary, something you have imagined that doesn't exist or hasn't happened.

**Limits** - A point or level which cannot be passed.

**Senses** - What we use to see, hear, feel, taste, smell and sense things.

**Species** - A group of similar and related organisms.

**Vast** - Very big.

# BOOKS BY EMMA APPLE

**The Best Selling Children's First Questions Series:**
Book 1: How Big Is Allah?
Book 2: How Does Allah Look?
Book 3: Where Is Allah?
Book 4: Is Allah Real?

**The Owl and Cat Series:**
Owl & Cat: Ramadan Is...
Owl & Cat: Islam Is...
Owl & Cat: Family Is...

Find more from Emma Apple online at www.emmaapple.com

Made in the USA
Middletown, DE
19 May 2018